MW01245526

Esraa Saad is a Saudi poet, and author of two poetry books. She self-published her first poetry book, *Beneath the Surface*, at the age of nineteen, and soon followed her second poetry book, *Lost Letters*. The author has been writing since childhood, finding poetry in love, loss, and the meaning of life making it relevant to all readers of poetry.

Esraa Saad

THE HEAVY FEATHERS

AUSTIN MACAULEY PUBLISHERS™

LONDON · CAMBRIDGE · NEW YORK · SHARJAH

ISBN 9789948801122 (Paperback)
ISBN 9789948801139 (E-Book)

Application Number: MC-10-01-9744074
Age Classification: E

First Published 2023
AUSTIN MACAULEY PUBLISHERS FZE
Sharjah Publishing City
P.O Box [519201]
Sharjah, UAE
www.austinmacauley.ae
+971 655 95 202

I would like to give a special thank you to my parents for always believing in me. A great appreciation to my beloved family for always supporting me throughout this journey. Special recognition to my dearest friends for staying by my side even when at times I didn't make it easy.

Table of Contents

Graceful Flowers   9

Tidal Waves   10

Write You   11

Confessions   12

When Battles Choose Us   14

War   15

My Last Sentiment   16

The Abyss   17

Nature's Beauty   18

Human   19

Unfamiliar Ground   20

Ocean   21

Revolving Door   22

The Illiterate   23

The Possessive Kind   24

Delirium   26

Wide Open   27

The Butterflies Are Killing Me   28

The Sun Never Fails to Shine   29

Lifeguard   30

Note to the World   31

Ripeness   32

Birds in Golden Cages   33

Maps   34

Living with Desolation   35

Symptoms   36

Gardens   37

Hidden Triggers   38

Fickle Hearts   40

The A Generation   41

Gentle Victories   42

My Almost   43

Only at Night   44

Within the Lines   45

Sidelines   47

Leap of Faith   48

Good Girl   49

"I Write on Water What I Dare Not Say"   50

The Martyr   51

Graceful Flowers

I promised my mother
to always have grace
the way flowers bloom
even when their heavy
petals are withering away
in an elegant vase
sinking in dirty water
without enough room
for me to breathe.
I put on a brave face
but, I'm too afraid to bother
so, I dial back the volume
and try to fold my body
to take up little space
where I sit in the corner
of every room I walk into.
If well behaved women rarely
make history, then I've barely left a trace
when being quiet is my shelter
within this dark hollow gloom.
I'm nothing more than the shadow behind me
for graceful flowers don't have a voice.

Tidal Waves

Darling, you are like tidal waves,
depending on the time and day,
caught between your mood swings,
never know if this time you'll stay,
or storm away and cut all strings.
I constantly wait across the bay,
until your next waves of emotions,
splash on me and wash away,
all the love and patience,
and all I'm left with is this heartache.

Write You

I tried to write you out,
but every time I pen you down,
there are no teardrops to dry,
no veins to bleed
on pages that have grown hungry for stains.
Only empty papers,
can reflect the way I feel,
no heartache to heal.
I'm stuck inside a hallway with nothing to weigh at both ends,
leaving caught me before I could decide.
I cannot force this discontent to settle with the guilt,
that's been taking place inside my chest.
My self-pity is mocking my pride,
for not taking a stand.
These empty papers are staring at me with judging eyes,
for the lines I couldn't fill out.
This is me letting go,
of all the time I wasted on nothingness.
I have no regrets,
but I cannot stretch my patience longer than this.
This is the white lie on empty lines,
the pretend-togetherness behind my smiles,
this is the last goodbye.

Confessions

The day you went away
I fell like autumn leaves from trees,
withered away,
and drifted away from the days.
Made a home out of this suitcase,
wandered the world to make me forget
the stinging pain of my present.
I ran away from reality,
when it was no longer holding you,
you said you wanted what's best for me,
but my heart was rooting for us two.
You're the only one who can save me,
From the darkness that surrounds me.
I know your bleeding heart is aching too,
but my heart is growing weary,
and it feels like winter inside my bones.
You took away my favorite seasons,
and left me here with the fall,
and the winter's cold.
I am writing this letter to tell you,
my eyes haven't run dry,
my lips haven't smiled in a while,
the waiting is breaking my heart,

time hasn't mended my wounds.
I cannot get over you.

When Battles Choose Us

They say choose your battles,
but every day, I wake up bruised,
from all the beating I did not choose,
crippled by my own shackles,
weighing me down every time I move.
My comfort zone is uncomfortable,
it's full of voices setting me up to lose.
Everyday feels like a war against barriers,
where I keep pushing my way through
roads of dying dreams and doubtful
thoughts daring me to prove
myself to the point of emotional
distress and unresolved issues.
I don't know how to be gentle
with myself and my faltering moods.
I'm stuck in the middle of this struggle,
worn out by all my restrictions and rules.

War

I refuse to give in,
I refuse to let you in,
but, there's a bond between us,
one I cannot seem to break.
My hands are always trying to unwind,
everything that tries to tie me down,
and, I understand that this is what love is about,
but, I have grown too resistant to my feelings.
I've been in war for too long that I can't simply surrender,
I can't wave a white flag and hand over my heart,
even though your hands are made of heavenly cushions,
and they will guard it safe and sound.
I have seen too much that I think too little of this,
I know what heals me and I avoid it.
I avoid the only potion that will end my battle,
because then I will be at peace,
and, I'm at war when I'm most content under my skin.

My Last Sentiment

Perhaps, I have overstayed
my welcome in a relationship
that no longer serves respect.
Perhaps, the walls in this place
are falling like a sinking ship
while I'm desperately trying to resurrect
all the love and trust I have raised
at a home that was once full of vivid
memories and great intellect.
Perhaps that's the price I have paid
for staying out of habit
when all around me was long wrecked.
There is no more love nor hate
only you, standing indifferent
and just like sand, you slipped
away through my fingers.

The Abyss

I wasn't your first choice
I knew it from the day we met
yet I let you fall into me
and all you found was a vast void.
I thought I could be your safety net
instead, you fell into a dark empty
hole where the shattering noise
of the world becomes nonexistent.
I'm merely just a shell of body
where beautiful things get destroyed
full of obituary and regret.

Nature's Beauty

The lines across your face
are paths to every story
that took place
in your unfinished journey,
every heartache,
every pain
silver streaks and grey
have crowned you with grace.
Forget what they
have to say,
you don't have to explain,
your beauty
is not something to maintain.
Your beauty is dignity
in all the wisdom you've gained.
Your beauty is not bound by society
standards and not defined by your age.

Human

If I were a flower,
I want to blossom in plain sight.
If I were a candy,
I want to be flaunted by my flavor.
If I were a pearl,
I want to break free from my shell.
If I were a statue,
I want to stand in public rather than on a shelf.
If I were an image,
I want to represent myself.
If I were a shame,
I want to defend myself.
But I am a woman.
A human,
with flesh and bones.
I am a woman,
not a metaphor,
I am human,
With a heart and soul.

Unfamiliar Ground

Lately, I'm unraveling
something inside me
has awakened
something I cannot unsee
like a world of mayhem
crashed into my decrepit reality
where all balance was shaken
by a parallel line that suddenly
collided with all my convictions.
Here I am, desperately
clinging to my religion
or the resemblance of a holy
belief against all reason
with my lack of entreaty
in a prayer where my shivering
knees fall obediently
to the floor asking for nothing
but my sanity
praying that god will listen
before I finally disappear
for eternity.

Ocean

You're an ocean
I don't know how to swim against its current.
You know how to hold me gracefully,
But it's me who's afraid of drowning.
These flames are drawn to your shore,
Knowing they'll be overwhelmed by it,
Yet the fire in my heart
Has found comfort in the way
Your waves crash against it.
You've taught my legs
How to walk on water
And free myself under it,
Closer to me than my very own core,
I carry you everywhere I go.
The way seashells carry the ocean.
You spin me like a storm,
Cleansing the wreckage from my soul,
To wrap me in your warmth
Keeping the fire in my heart from fading,
And now my lungs have given up on air,
Because now you're the air I'm breathing.

Revolving Door

You spend your time
with the haunting notion
of always wanting more.
Life is passing you by
in fast motion
right before
your eager eyes.
You're too tired
chasing after recognition
and keeping score
with your toughest rival
staring back at you in the reflection
asking "What are you looking for?"
"Is it all worth the try?"
that is the question
and that is your downfall.
With endless attempts to satisfy
your longing for perfection
and a delirious mind.
Here you stand, an empty soul
looking back at your life
to realize it was nothing
but a revolving door.

The Illiterate

She may be fifty years late
with her wrinkled hand
writing down her fate
for the very first time
she refused to wait
to take this vital stand.
Perhaps misogyny is to blame
patriarchy, circumstance, or the man
she married managed to claim
her youth along with her plans.
There's no time left to waste
for she's finally holding her fate
in the palm of her wrinkled hand.

The Possessive Kind

You clipped my wings,
said it's for my own good.
You crippled my feet,
so that I can't find my own way.
You painted the streets,
with patterns of permanent stray.
Cut off all longing,
for past memories,
and all yearning,
for future discovery.
I am tied up in knots,
only you can solve them.
Blood-colored eyes,
unseeing from suffocation.
You offer me choices,
only to dissolve them with infused fears.
I am caught in a spider's web,
pulling my insides with a desperate consent.
I am sucked in too deep
that I don't know how to leave.
My free will is trapped inside your cave,
and I'm holding on to dreary traps.
If this will be my permanent grave,

I will turn to my basic instincts,
and drag my way back to common sense,
out of your ominous hands,
ragged to the point of never being used again.

Delirium

On most days
she feels as if though
her head is floating
in a foggy haze
tied to a thin rope
that keeps wandering
until she strays
from her self-control
and that's what she fears the most.

Wide Open

forgive me, if I'm being very sensitive
lately, all my wounds are exposed
and all my stricken feelings
are out demanding justice.
forgive me, if I'm easily provoked
when you pour your casual teasing
on my bruised ego with foolish
and inconsiderate words.
forgive me if I seem gutless
it's just that there is a hole
in my stomach for not dealing
with all my clenched punches
this is the aftermath of my passive
reactions becoming an erupting volcano.

The Butterflies Are Killing Me

the butterflies in my stomach turn
to knives cutting holes inside me
with a tenacious heartburn
each time you threaten to leave.
my heart has become a ticking bomb
at the mercy of your hand not to release
the pin while you carelessly go on
and leave me here to bleed.
I never knew abuse could be this calm
until it slowly stole away my safety.
Now I find myself torn
between my heart and my dignity.
If I stay, I will be staying out of fear,
and it will be death in another form
to settle for a life of eternal misery.

The Sun Never Fails to Shine

There are eight planets in this world
they all orbit around the sun
in a rapid succession
everyday a new sunlight is born
from her undivided attention
even the earth is drawn
towards her warmth
and igniting affection
and then there's the moon
reflecting her beauty from a distance
with a glowing passion
while the stars portray the perfect constellation
I guess what I'm trying to say
mother, you are the sun in this one

Lifeguard

You were my lifeguard
when I jumped in headfirst
into the vastness of life
reckless and immersed
through struggles and fights
and every lesson learned
you were there by my side
you never failed to immerse
always along for the ride
through the pain and the hurt
and the lows and highs
and even at my worst
you painted the blue sky
with rose colored
rays of sunlight
and you were my only constant
when everything went awry

Note to the World

I wonder if someone had stayed
that day you needed company
I wonder if the world wasn't too busy
they wouldn't be reading this note today
and you wouldn't be getting buried.

Ripeness

By the time you reach thirty
you will favor solitude
over barren company
and your arbitrary innocence
will be polished with maturity.
You will feel more gratitude
towards the hard decisions
that led to growth and stability
and aid in building you
with strength and integrity.
You will become immune
to what people have to say.
You will cherish your self-value
and free it from the prisons
of placing your worth in productivity
and fixed routines with hollow reviews.
You will learn to keep your distance
from people who disturb your peace
you will become someone who knows
how to enjoy the little moments
that make up the beautiful journey.

Birds in Golden Cages

they kept us sheltered
to keep us obedient
until we became disabled
believing in something insignificant.
We walk this earth pretending
our wings aren't burdens forced
upon us by their ancient
beliefs that scourged us
from birth until this present.
Our heavy wings fluttered
despite our desperate attempts
we couldn't fly, so we floated
the sky trying to reach the summit.
We fell, stumbled, and we wandered
the world with great content
knowing that even free birds fly in herd
and that's what made us different.

Maps

You pin words on my body
with tokens and call it your continent.
You discover new territories
and call them your monuments
while you place your victory
flags on every segment.
You expand your perpetual traveling
on rivers of veins you have won
to write your lustrous history
of boastful victories
as your discovered regents
and call me yours for eternity.

Living with Desolation

Grief clings to her
like a chronic illness.
Manifesting on her figure
the harsh traces of reminiscence
the smell of death lingers
on her skin with bitterness
guilt hides behind her laughter
like the ghost of a haunting mistress
she can't escape this nightmare
until the melancholy darkness
dissolves with all the anger
leaving her with the broken pieces
that no longer fit together.

Symptoms

I wake up with this burden
like having to go to a funeral
of all my loved ones
but I'm too tired to mourn
I would rather be in denial
than feel anything at all
my mind grasps for motivation
my body is in constant withdrawal
fighting the hands of gravitation
just to be able to stand tall
I carry the tragedies of this enervating
world like it's my inherent fault
I drag my feet with hesitation
like it's my natural default
to feel immensely broken
losing myself with every cycle
this is what it's like to have depression
from someone who looks normal

Gardens

I have loved you in small doses
I couldn't grasp you all at once
you were softly nestled inside my heart
where you have grown thousands of roses
seeds to gardens spared within my lungs
built evergreen trees in the courtyard
of my weak feeble bones
walked through the darkness
and shed light into my broken parts
held open my soul before it closes
forever with all my dreams and hopes
and put to rest all my wounds and scars

Hidden Triggers

Hallow,
That's all she feels
every time she swallows
a bite from her rationed meals
tongue thrusting with sorrow
every particle of energy she needs
perhaps this time she will let go
and live the moment before she disappears
inside a wasted bag of bones
while she goes on to conceal
her tired face and sore throat
numbers and mirrors continue to steal
her worth and replace it with self-loathe
Every day begins with dying leaves
exorcising the nourishment from her soul
while she continues to feed
on motivation in the form of shooting arrows
aimed at the lack of gap between
her legs, that dangle like shadows
she enforces discipline with extreme
measurements and self-control
of all the things she cannot reveal
her striking collarbones

are a serious scream
of all the pain underneath her clothes

Fickle Hearts

I did not lose you
nor you lost me
there was nothing
enough to hold onto
the ground beneath us was shaky
our feet were reeling
like we somehow outgrew
walking and completely
lost ourselves in this spin
we call love or perhaps our lost value
to be admired without legacy
or even be part of something
deeper than our virtue
while the effects of gravity
kept missing
us, we finally fell through
the cracks of reality
back into existential suffering
where I am me and you are you
nothing out of the ordinary

The A Generation

Endless sleepless nights
mornings running on coffee
trying to survive
in a ruthless economy
children in disguise
behind false ideology
struggling to thrive
in a world overrun by technology
moving in a constant overdrive
to pursue the fantasy of success stories
and the illusion of the high life
where happiness equals money
while the ultimate price
is the degeneration of humanity
they continue to roll the dice
on these wasted empty
days they call their lives
with goals infused with anxiety
that's the glaring prize
of this generation's prodigy
young beautiful minds
slowly dying of apathy

Gentle Victories

Stop waiting for an apology
from people who know
very little about being sorry.
Stop needing them to show
support and sympathy
for everything you go through.
And most importantly
stop expecting them to owe
you anything for your humanity.
The love you give will grow
inside you like a weeping tree
rivers of compassion will flow
like gentle victories over enemies
and you will no longer be in the shadow
of expectations or feel the need
for validation and gratitude.

My Almost

You are a warm breeze on a cold winter
you are that last anticipated sip
of coffee on a Sunday morning
you are that expensive leather
jacket on my wish list
you are that diamond ring
I wish to place on my finger
you are that last clip
of a classic movie ending
I would solemnly watch forever
you are that last lit
cigarette, slowly burning
in the hand of a heavy smoker
you are the words that never left my lips
when it was time to say something
You are my almost happy ever after
and that is the closest
I've ever gotten to dying

Only at Night

I lock the door at night
keep my windows
shut very tight
hold my pillow close
lose myself in the white
noise of the raindrops
and the thunder light.
For a moment time stops
tears fall from my eyes
I see a glimpse of shadow
and then I realize
I'm still haunted by the ghost of you.

Within the Lines

Your love is conditional,
depending on the season,
whether the flowers blossom,
or turn pale and feeble,
you hold me under your thumb,
while I seek your approval,
like a terrified victim,
afraid to cause any trouble,
with my feelings numb,
and my words careful.
Your love is conditional,
that it cost me my freedom,
I fear the day will come,
when I become resentful,
and you will be the reason.
Your condescending dismissal,
is worse than a loaded gun,
shooting bullets with cynical
words behind constructive criticism.
Your love is conditional,
that I fear the day will come,
when my actual
existence will no longer be welcome,

if I don't live up to your version
of all my wasted potential.
And all this time I wasted seeking your validation,
has left me empty and miserable.

Sidelines

You live life like a flat line
with a monotonous heartbeat
watching life pass you by
like being stuck in the backseat
living is not the same as getting by
learn to have a little greed
while you passively live on this high
state of mind that seems a lot like defeat
you're passed reading the signs
on these endless lonely streets
with nowhere to go but drive
aimlessly trying to achieve
something worth this ride
as the days become weeks
and even the deep blue sky
becomes a giant wrapping sheet
slowly suffocating the life
out of your hopes and dreams
while you are stuck on sidelines
full of regret and defeat

Leap of Faith

Let's move forward
to the moment
we're passed awkward
stares and stolen
glances waiting to be harbored
let's pretend our hearts were never broken
and our souls were never shattered
let's set our hearts in motion
and let our spirts flirt
with the dangers of free falling
where we would rather be scattered
than settle for a life of limitation

Good Girl

Sit still, hush, hush little girl,
tuck your knees and lower your voice,
you are not meant to conquer the world,
you will always be less than boys,
so, scour your sharp edges into soft swirls.
Do your chores but keep your hands moist,
For you are a cherished pearl.
So, fold your bones and bend your joints,
inside this dark lonely shell.
For, good girls don't have a choice,
but to behave on society's terms,
away from all the noise,
undisrupted by the movement's efforts,
to regain your worth,
too busy trying to avoid,
any conflict with the world.
Good girls living in a wasted void,
waiting to be filled.

"I Write on Water What I Dare Not Say"

for I am the mother and daughter,
of misfortunate disarray,
the swirls are getting bigger,
while the fringe is starting to fray,
with my teeth grinding harder,
and all the things I have to say,
spiral into the deep water,
as I watch the remains,
reach the surface changed in color,
like a blood-red blaze,
exploding from the pressure,
and I burn to ashes in flames,
"I write on water
what I dare not say",
will be written on the center,
of my grave.

The Martyr

she didn't apprehend the struggle
of holding someone vulnerable
she didn't fathom how desperate
her hands were to find a heartbeat
in the veins of ever so fragile
vessels, so she whispered biblical
words and breathed life into his chest
but he was looking for an exit
her lips sent an electric ripple
with her desperate attempts of revival
but his beautiful warm spirit
was long gone and this was his last visit
she never knew what she was capable
of until she had to put him to rest